Ploughman

Immigrant

Farmer

One Man's Pursuit of the American Dream

John Borrowman

BAY CREEK PUBLISHING

PLOUGHMAN, IMMIGRANT, FARMER
August 2016

Cover design by Jason Hapney, Horton Group.
Interior design by David K. Dodd.

Library of Congress Control Number 2016944674

ISBN 978-0-9835670-8-0

Published by
Bay Creek Publishing
PO Box 546
Fish Creek, WI 54212

**Dedicated to
Carroll Borrowman**

Preface

In our modern world, families are separated by greater and greater distances. The greater the distance, it seems, the more our human nature pushes us to connect to a common story. That connection was once made through oral history. Today, story-telling happens more often in a book.

This book is the story of my great-great-great grandfather, John Borrowman. He brought his wife and nine children from Scotland to America in 1838. Over the course of his life, he was a ploughman, an immigrant, and finally a farmer.

You might think that writing someone's story is a pretty straightforward project; simply a matter of connecting the dots. Depending on the life you're examining, though, some dots can be faint or even non-existent. If you're lucky, you start with a few dots and by turning them in the kaleidoscope so to speak, you see new dots. By considering how individuals act in similar situations, you can assume even more dots.

These are flesh-and-blood people, though, with thoughts and feelings about where they went and what they did. They are not people to whom life simply *happened*. To tell their story more fully, I reached beyond the dots to capture those thoughts and feelings. That is why I call it a "re-constructed family story."

John Borrowman
Summer 2016

Ploughman

There was a time in history when land wasn't owned. Land was conquered, lived on and sometimes lost to the enemy. But, never owned. Never bought or sold. Sooner or later, that began to change in different ways in different places around the world.

It changed in Scotland when a king decided he would give land to soldiers who helped him stay in power. That king was David I, who was crowned King of Scotland in 1124. The soldiers were Knights who brought armies with them when they came to Scotland from France, about the time David took the throne.

Each grant of land that King David made carried with it an obligation or feu (as in feudalism). The person who received the grant had the right to subdivide the land and grant it again to another, further down the chain. Each subsequent grant also carried its own feu. The Knights' original feu was military service on behalf of the King. As the land was divided and granted yet again, the feu came to include goods, services, and cash.

The land passed from son to son to son. It was sometimes lost or won in battle and even reclaimed by the king to reward his new favorites. Despite seven hundred years of changes since David's reign, that land—and the wealth and power that went with it—remained in the grip of a small circle of very powerful men.

Any man outside that circle who wanted to plow his own ground could only dream. John Borrowman was one of those dreamers.

* * *

One Man's Pursuit of the American Dream

John was born in Dolphinton, Scotland, December 21, 1788, a cold, cold Sunday. A hard freeze had set in across the country on November 30 and didn't lift until early the next year. The same bitter weather reached London, four hundred miles to the south, where it froze the river Thames thick enough to support the crowds that came out to enjoy a winter fair set up on the ice.

Back in Dolphinton, the birth of a baby was guaranteed to bring neighbors out of their homes on a cold December day. With the women who had come to attend John's mother, along with his father, his twelve-year-old sister, Catharine, and ten-year-old brother, Hugh, the tiny home must have been filled with activity.

Dolphinton is a village located in a parish by the same name. When John was born, it was no more than a few homes and outbuildings spread thinly along either side of the road connecting the towns of Edinburgh, twenty-one miles to the northeast, and Biggar, seven miles southwest. (Map 1) Dolphinton sits where the land flattens out just beyond the southwestern tail of the Pentland Hills. On the northwest side of Dolphinton, a massive lump known as the Black Mount rises about 1500 feet above the rolling terrain. The Mount was originally carved by ice age glaciers that advanced, and then receded. Eons of wind and weather have left it looking like a giant's thumb and forefinger pinched a few acres of land into a great bulge.

John's family hadn't always lived in Dolphinton. His father, Andrew Borrowman, was born August 12, 1744, in Dunsyre Parish, just north of Dolphinton Parish on the opposite side of the Black Mount. Both Dunsyre and Dolphinton parishes are in Lanarkshire. Andrew was the oldest of four children of John Borrowman and Agnes Thripland. While the best evidence is that Andrew's wife (John's mother), Janet Thomson, came from the village of West Linton, about 10 miles ESE of Dunsyre Parish, conflicting records leave us uncertain about her birth date, parents, or siblings.

Ploughman

How and when Andrew and Janet met is unknown, but they were married August 3, 1776. Catharine was their first-born, May 18, 1777. Hugh arrived almost two and a half years later, October 10, 1779. Both Catharine and Hugh were born when the family was living in Broughton Parish, which is in Peebleshire, and about seven miles due south from Andrew's birthplace in Dunsyre Parish. (Map 2) At some point, the family moved north back across the border into Lanarkshire where John was born in the village of Dolphinton on that cold December day.

* * *

Today, John would be considered an "almost-Christmas" baby. In 1788, he wasn't. Christmas wasn't celebrated in his home, or in any of the homes around Dolphinton. Or any Protestant homes anywhere in Scotland, for that matter. Almost one hundred fifty years earlier, in 1640, the Church of Scotland had strong-armed the Scottish Parliament into banning the celebration of Christmas because it was a religious festival of the then-hated Catholic Church and its Pope. More broadly, the Church of Scotland also made it a point to stand firmly against fun and frivolity. (It wasn't until 1954 that Christmas was officially declared a public holiday in Scotland.)

However, Dolphinton villagers didn't skip celebrations altogether. New Year's Eve was the favored holiday and was (and still is) called Hogmanay. The Church also looked on Hogmanay disapprovingly, but in the end likely turned a blind eye because celebrating the arrival of the New Year was so deeply rooted in ancient social customs.

John's baptism was January 11, 1790, four weeks to the day from when he was born. Because it was a Sunday, his parents probably took him to the parish church for the ceremony. We can't be sure, though. Ministers sometimes performed the rites in the newborn's home. In any case,

Dolphinton Parish records contain a short note, scrawled in a florid hand, confirming the event.

Excerpt from Dolphinton Parish Records

John, son to Andrew Borrowman indweller Gateside and Janet Thomson his spouse born Decr 21st 1788 and baptized Janry 11th 1789 witnesses to said baptism George Ferguson Tennant Roberton mains and William Paterson Tennant Dolphinton.

Scotland had powerful landowners at that time, but very little governmental structure. By default, the Church was the civil authority throughout the country. That made parish records *the* legal records. It also made them the *only* records for many people so poor that their names were recorded nowhere else. John's parents were in that category.

While the Dolphinton Parish record doesn't tell us whether John's baptism happened at home or at church, it does tell us that George Ferguson and William Paterson were on hand as witnesses. Paterson was a labourer living in the village. Ferguson was the tenant (overseer) at Roberton Mains, one of the farms on Dolphinton Estate.

John's father, Andrew Borrowman, was a cottar—a farm labourer whose wages included a cottage with a small plot of land to grow food for his family, along with grazing rights for what little stock he could afford. On the socio-economic ladder, a cottar stood on one of the lowest rungs.

Although parish records were the only records for many of the poor, that didn't mean they were complete, or even accurate. Birth dates were recorded only in connection with baptism. And baptisms went into the record only because *clergy* performed the ceremony. Marriages were recorded for much the same reason. Burials of nearly everyone except the wealthiest were usually handled by the surviving family, without involvement by the church. As a result, deaths were recorded far less often.

In October 1792, when John was nearly four, his mother had twins, David and Adam. In a time when large families were more the rule, there is no record of any additional children born to Andrew Borrowman and Janet Thomson. Further, there is no record of the marriage of either twin, David or Adam. Could it be that they died young?

The church's job as civil record-keeper originated when only monks could read and write. After the arrival of the Reformation in the 1500s, the church *also* considered itself the keeper of a moral code. In each parish, responsibility for enforcing that code fell to the Kirk Session, which was a committee of two elders and the minister.

Human nature being what it is, unwed mothers-to-be and their paramours were a convenient target of the church's attention. Offenders were summoned to appear before the Kirk Session for judgment. The usual penalty was to sit on the "stool of repentance" and be rebuked by the minister in front of the congregation for several Sundays.

In addition to enforcing the moral code, the Kirk Session managed the financial affairs of the parish church. Drifters who came to the church for help were deemed paupers and sent on their way, sometimes with transportation paid in hopes of sending the problem somewhere else. While dismissing the paupers, the Session did see fit to authorize quarterly payments of £1 each (about $80 today) to widows who they considered the deserving poor.

Stool of repentance

By the time John grew to be a young man, the church had all but given up its public finger-wagging at moral miscreants.

* * *

Dolphinton Parish was a religious unit, whereas Dolphinton Estate was commercial. Though their respective territories did not fully overlap, together, they touched the lives of everyone in the area. The parish church gave spiritual comfort to the people and was the source of civil government and order that benefited the estate. For its part, the estate helped fund the church and was the engine that drove the financial life of the area.

The church's role had developed largely in reaction to social circumstances. The estate, on the other hand, had evolved over centuries of complex and deliberately controlled land ownership arrangements. Those arrangements were part and parcel of the Scotland that John was born into, and one of the reasons that thousands like him went to America.

John's home village of Dolphinton—together with the parish and estate around it—is said to take its name from Dolfine, a nobleman who dominated this part of Scotland in the 11th century. The reality of any actual connection between Dolfine and Dolphinton is lost to history. A faint trail of ownership of the estate does run back to the clan of Douglas and beyond, to men that rallied with Scotland's hero, Robert the Bruce, who drove the English out of Scotland in 1314. Taking the connection back even further, Bruce himself was descended from one of the Knights who came from France and received grants of land from King David.

By the 1600s, however, control of Dolphinton Estate was in the hands of the Browns. Kenneth Mackenzie married into the Brown family in 1755 and eventually became Laird of the estate. Kenneth's grandson, Richard Mackenzie, was the Laird at the time John was a boy.

Ploughman

Of the 2400 acres of the estate, almost 1800 acres were spread across six farms ranging in size from 133 acres to nearly 700 acres. Each farm was managed by a tenant who signed a nineteen-year lease, known as a tack. The nineteen-year term was fairly standard as John grew up. It recognized that the tenant needed time to recoup his investment in improvements to the farm. The tack also included a concession to cottars like John's father, Andrew—labourers with a little acreage for livestock—which allowed them to cut the sod for building fences and covering the roofs of their cottages.

John grew up in a cottage like this

In addition to cash rent, the tenant was obliged to deliver to the Laird's house as many as a dozen hens and thirty carts of coal each year, depending on the size of his farm. A few smaller plots of land large enough for a house, and perhaps a garden or a few livestock, were rented by other individuals for cash and similar requirements of hens and coal.

Today, the Laird's annual rental income would be just over $115,000.

* * *

By the time John was ten, the population in Dolphinton Parish had dropped to about 200, from nearly 300 reported just fifty years earlier. The *Old Statistical Account*, published in 1799 and written by Reverend John Gordon, minister of Dolphinton Parish, gives us a clue to why. Gordon points the finger at landowners who were increasing their acreage (and their income) by repossessing smaller parcels that they had formerly set aside for cottars and their families.

As a man of the cloth, Gordon's sympathies are clear when he writes that "now the farms are much enlarged, and the farmers, at least many of them, seem to have imbibed a strong prejudice against all cottages, pulling down some of them every year." Without a place to live, Gordon claimed, people simply left the area.

Rev. Gordon's account includes a census of the parish showing that of the total population, fifty were in John's age group (ten years and younger). At the other end of the age continuum, there were fifteen people who were seventy years and older. Gordon's census catalogs a blacksmith and a mason, along with several carpenters and weavers. In a statistic that reveals the level of poverty, there were no shoemakers or tailors. Villagers probably couldn't afford to buy new shoes. Clothes were made and mended at home.

The good news in the report was Rev. Gordon's estimate that twenty to thirty young people were enrolled in school. John was probably one of them. Even so, a Bible was the only book in homes like his. It wouldn't have occurred to John that the Laird had his own library with works in French, German and Latin—languages John wouldn't have recognized anyway. Even more evidence for where he stood in the pecking order.

John was eleven at the turn of the century in 1800. Outside the isolated world of Dolphinton, the Industrial Revolution was gaining steam. In America, Eli Whitney had recently invented the cotton gin. Barely twenty miles west of Dolphinton, the mills at New Lanark were running faster and faster to meet the demand for cotton fabric. In an unusual social experiment, the mills provided housing for workers and education for their children. At the same time, the mills made it harder and harder for individual weavers like those in Dolphinton to make a living.

Ploughman

* * *

John's name first appeared in the Dolphinton Parish records in connection with his baptism in 1789. Thirty years passed before it appeared again. The occasion was his wedding: June 11, 1819. His bride was Jean Ormiston.

At some point in the two decades between the turn of the century and his wedding, John went to work as a ploughman, or hired-hand, at Meadowhead, one of the farms on Dolphinton Estate. Farm labourer wages were seven to ten shillings a week (about $55 today). William Brown was the tenant at Meadowhead and stood as a witness at John Borrowman's wedding. The other witness at the wedding was the bride's brother, John Ormiston, who was John Borrowman's co-worker at Meadowhead and most likely the matchmaker who brought husband and wife together.

Labourers like Borrowman and Ormiston worked under six-month contracts. They renewed their contracts—or sought out new employers—during one of the semi-annual community fairs held on Whitsunday (seventh Sunday after Easter) and Martinmas (around November 11). Both holidays had originated in the church, though they had lost much of their religious connection over the years and had become opportunities primarily for general socializing.

John Ormiston and his sister, Jean, were the oldest and youngest, respectively, of four children born to Thomas Ormiston and Elisabeth Conquor at Morham Parish in East Lothian, some forty-seven miles east of Dolphinton. **(Map 3)** It's a puzzle as to why John and Jean traveled so far from home. Lives were more commonly lived much closer to the place of birth. (For example, Andrew Borrowman and his wife, Janet Thomson, never lived more than twelve miles from either's birthplace.) Though the puzzle is incomplete, we have enough pieces to help us get a sense of their motivation.

Apparently, the two of them came to stay with a distant relative named Helen Ormiston in Newland Parish, which bordered Dolphinton Parish to the southeast. Records are too sparse to confirm exactly how John and Jean were related to Helen. Our only clue is that John and Jean share last names with Helen, and that Helen was from Midlothian, the shire (county) that bordered East Lothian, where John and Jean were born.

Helen Ormiston had married William Gibson in January 1817. Their first child, a daughter named Agnes, was born the following October. The picture that emerges is that Jean Ormiston may have come to help care for the baby and John came along with the intention of finding work.

John Ormiston did eventually hire on at Meadowhead Farm, in Dolphinton, where room and board were part of his pay. Jean continued to live with Helen and William in Newland Parish until her marriage in 1819. The ruins of the parish church still sit, surrounded by teetering gravestones, just up the hill from a clear-running creek named Lyne Water.

Twenty years after Jean's marriage to John Borrowman, Helen Ormiston and William Gibson were an important connection for them in America.

* * *

John Borrowman was twenty-nine when he married Jean Ormiston. She was sixteen. Marriage at such a young age was not uncommon for women in early 19th century Scotland. The newlyweds set up house in a rented room at Logiebank, where the local schoolmaster lived. Logiebank stood on four acres of land donated in 1650 by the Laird of Dolphinton Estate as a place to build a home for the schoolmaster. (**Map 4**)

John and Jean's first son, Andrew, was born at Logiebank, February 24, 1820. As was the custom, John had been named after his grandfather, and so had Andrew. The child was baptized March 19. Witnesses were the same William

Ploughman

Brown and John Ormiston, who stood with John and Jean at their wedding the previous June.

John Borrowman had a ten-minute walk from Logiebank to his job at Meadowhead. His route took him about a hundred yards south down a gentle incline, and then east-northeast along Biggar Road for another two hundred yards. At that point, he turned south again and followed an S-curved lane leading to Meadowhead Farm.

John probably had no idea that the stretch of Biggar Road he walked every day was originally laid by the Romans who fought their way north from London into this part of Scotland about AD 71. The Romans scuffled with native tribes and finally retreated south into Great Britain about AD 211. For John, the road was nothing more than his path to work.

* * *

John and Jean's first son, Andrew, was just over a year old when they had a second son, Robert, born April 1, 1821. Robert's baptism was three weeks later, April 22, enough time for William Gibson and Helen Ormiston, whom Jean had lived with back in Newland Parish, to travel to Dolphinton for the ceremony. Gibson was a witness, along with Jean's brother, John Ormiston. Ormiston and Borrowman still worked together at Meadowhead.

John and Jean's young family of four was crammed into their tiny space at Logiebank. If they were going to improve their situation, John's ploughman's wages would have to go further. Wages have always been a topic of conversation among co-workers. It probably was no different on Dolphinton Estate. As workers saw each other, information was traded in quick snatches of conversation, and John might have heard that he could make more at Roberton Mains—another of the farms on the estate—where Hugh Gilbert was now the tenant.

Because Meadowhead was the "home farm," much of what it produced ended up on the Laird's table. Here John grew crops that he fed to chickens, cattle and sheep. He gathered eggs, milked cows, and churned butter. Little of Meadowhead's output was sold to the market. By contrast, Roberton Mains was farmed mostly in the interest of selling to the market. There John would have spent more time herding and shearing sheep for wool to be sold for profits, giving the tenant the ability to pay a higher wage.

Roberton Mains was situated about three-quarters of a mile up a lane that ran north from Biggar Road and passed alongside the Dolphinton Parish Church. **(Map 4)** At just under 300 acres, Roberton was the second largest farm on Dolphinton Estate and generated about £340 (just over $41,000 today) in annual cash rent to the Laird, along with the hens and coal that Gilbert was required to deliver to the Laird under his tack (lease).

John might have had an inside track on a job at Roberton Mains through his brother-in-law, Thomas Cleghorn, who also worked there. Cleghorn was married to John's sister, Catharine. Though there is no parish record of their marriage, Thomas and Catharine declared themselves spouses when their son, David, was born in May 1816. They later had a daughter named Janet, born October 1819.

Cleghorn was in a position to put in a good word for John with Hugh Gilbert, the tenant at Roberton Mains. At the same time, tenants who ran the farms on the estate would have had their own grapevine. So, if John hadn't earned a good reputation as a hard worker at Meadowhead, Gilbert would have heard about it.

John talked with Gilbert, perhaps at one of the semi-annual festivals where hiring usually happened, and eventually left Meadowhead Farm to go to work at Roberton Mains. It's likely that his wages included living quarters with more room for his growing family. The change came none too soon for John and Jean. On September 12, 1822, they had a third son, Hugh. It's reasonable speculation that John named this third son in memory of his brother. In 1822, John's brother, Hugh, would have been forty-three. But, no records can be found that tell us what may have happened to brother Hugh—had he married, had children, or died at an early age?

John and Jean had their fourth son in mid-winter, early 1824. Born January 9, baby Thomas was named for Jean's father, Thomas Ormiston. Young Thomas was baptized January 24. John arranged for Thomas Colson, another of his co-workers at Roberton Mains, and William Crawford, who lived in a cottage on the farm, to come to the ceremony as witnesses. John continued to work at Roberton Mains while Jean managed the household and four boys, the oldest of which was only four years old. Jean might have had help from her sister-in-law, Catharine, who still lived in the area. Catharine was 26 years older than Jean and would have been a stabilizing influence. Catharine's six-year-old daughter, Janet, might have pitched in to help her Aunt Jean.

Near the end of 1824, John and Jean learned they would have a fifth child. Another boy, David, was born August 24, 1825. David got his name from John's younger brother, who was a twin to Adam. By the time David was born, Lockhart Stodart had taken over as the tenant at Roberton Mains. Stodart came from a wealthy family with holdings in Dunsyre Parish, on the other side of the Black Mount. Stodart showed John the kindness of standing as a witness for David's baptism. Thomas Colson was the second witness.

The financial pressure of providing for five children continued to mount. And still more children were born. On March 16, 1827, about a month before Easter, John and Jean had their sixth child and named him John, after John's grandfather. The baby's christening was April 3. Then, after ten years of marriage and the births of six boys, John and Jean finally had a girl. They named her Agnes, for both

John's grandmother and aunt. Agnes was born July 8, 1829, and baptized July 24.

Parish records for the baptisms of newborns John and Agnes refer to their father, John, only as a labourer in Dolphinton, leaving us to wonder which farm he might have worked on. Logically, he had to find the best wages he could. With seven children to feed, John Borrowman had one of the largest families in Dolphinton.

In 1829, when Agnes was born, John was forty. Jean was twenty-six. From this point forward, all trace of them disappears from the records of any parish. The remainder of their life in Scotland is a mystery.

* * *

Providing for his family had to have strained John's meager wages as a labourer. Perhaps he and Jean turned to family in the way others have done before and since. But John's family would have had nothing to offer. His father, Andrew, even if he were alive, would have been eighty-six. Alternatively, facts point toward John and Jean's turning to *her* family for help.

In Morham Parish to the east, Jean's father, Thomas Ormiston, would have been only fifty-six and better able to take them in. Jean's sister, Margaret, would have been twenty-six. An extra pair of hands—Margaret's—would have been useful in caring for the seven children. Still, we don't know what actually happened to John and Jean's young family during this time.

Interestingly, later records tell us that John and Jean had nine children, not seven. So, another mystery surrounds the births of George and Adam, their last two sons, because their birth and baptism records cannot be found. If the family had stayed in Dolphinton, we would expect to find parish records there for these two brothers just like for their siblings. On the other hand, if John and Jean moved somewhere else, how do we explain why parents who took such care to ar-

14

range baptisms for their first seven would not do the same for their last two children, no matter where they were living? Or were the records simply lost?

There is no evidence for when, or how, but at some point, John and his family made the decision to go to America. Letters from those who had already gone told stories of the brighter future awaiting those who came next if they were willing to work hard. Perhaps John heard the stories. Intuitively he knew he would never farm his own land in Scotland. His future was not in his homeland. It was in America.

Making the decision to go to America was difficult, but the harder part for the family of eleven would be *paying* for the trip. They faced a two-hundred-mile trek by foot and wagon from Scotland to the port of Liverpool, England, followed by a month's sail across the Atlantic before they would set foot in America. How could John do that on a ploughman's wages? A clue from the family's journey across America points to financial help from an unexpected source, and an arrangement involving one of John and Jean's children.

Immigrant

Life at the Port of Liverpool was ruled by the wind. When the wind wasn't right, ships didn't sail. If ships didn't sail, captains and sailors didn't get paid. Innkeepers were the only ones happy when the wind was still. The winds blew favorably on April 21, 1838. Forty-one ships left Liverpool that Saturday headed for ports all over the world. One of them was the St. Lawrence, bound for New York under the command of Oliver Brown. John Borrowman and his family of eleven had purchased tickets in steerage, and their lives were about to change forever.

Ships at Liverpool docks, c. 1841

The Emigrant's Guide, written and published by William Cobbett in 1829, reported steerage fare from Liverpool to New York to be 4 pounds 10 shillings (just over $500 today). As expensive as the price would be for John's family of eleven, steerage fares had once been much higher. They had fallen three decades earlier because of an odd confluence of events involving Napoleon Bonaparte.

In the late 1700s and early 1800s, Britain was in the midst of a building boom that fueled the demand for lumber harvested from forests around the Baltic Sea. In 1806, Napoleon negotiated alliances with Baltic powers that closed the Baltic Sea to British trade. In response, timber suppliers turned their attention across the Atlantic to Canada, which had vast forests of its own. Unwilling to let their ships sail empty to Canada, freight companies began to outfit their holds with crude wooden berths hammered together for human cargo and removed to make room for timber on the return trip to Britain. Fares were steeply discounted, and immigration to America got a massive boost. The surge in passengers encouraged investors to build more ships. The St. Lawrence was likely one of them.

To be insurable, ships had to be licensed through Lloyd's Register in England. The record for the St. Lawrence indicates she was built in 1821 in Montreal, Canada, and was intended for the North Atlantic trade. There is evidence that she was

Sailing ship like the St. Lawrence

captained by Oliver Brown on multiple crossings. Over 85 feet long and 25 feet at its widest point, the St. Lawrence had two main masts plus a tri-sail mast. She had a square-stern and was built in a carvel planking style, which let her carry more sail and have a broader hull. Captain Brown hired 15 – 20 sailors to crew the St. Lawrence.

* * *

John and his wife Jean prepared for their trip as best they could, relying on advice wherever they could get it. They took only what they could carry: clothes and food. Of the two, *food* was the clear priority. Some ship captains supplied food and levied an additional cost of 30 shillings per person (about $125 today). With eleven mouths to feed, John and Jean had no choice but to take their own.

Cobbett suggested to readers of his Emigrant's Guide that they take "flour, rice, ginger, candles, groats (oats), salt, pepper, vinegar, dried ham, other bacon, potatoes, butter, sugar, coffee, tea." Though he never liked biscuits, he noted that they could be valuable, not only as a foodstuff but an investment. Take more than you needed, Cobbett advised, and you could sell or bargain them later in the journey to passengers who hadn't planned as carefully.

Like everyone in steerage, John's family had one goal when they reached Liverpool: buy passage on the next ship leaving for America. Waiting would only drain precious cash. Any relief John felt once the St. Lawrence got underway disappeared when he thought about the reality of the step he had taken. He was leaving Scotland forever and taking his family to a foreign country. There was plenty of uncertainty. John had one advantage, however, as he left his home country. Tucked safely away in his belongings was a piece of paper bearing the name of a man in Cincinnati who would help them as they made their way toward St. Louis.

Not long after they came on board, John and Jean turned to the task of arranging their family's belongings in a vain attempt to claim some privacy. There were one hundred seventeen souls packed into steerage and privacy was at a premium. Blankets and bed sheets were hung to block the view, but *nothing* could block the constant sounds or unpleasant smells. Seasickness overwhelmed nearly all the passengers during the first week to ten days, though most everyone adjusted by the two-week mark.

Life in steerage was challenging enough on a good day. During a storm it was *miserable.* It was Brown's job to understand the storms his ship was bound to meet and to convey confidence to his sailors that they would ride out any peril. John and his steerage mates weren't nearly so confident. When heavy weather hit, hatches were closed, shutting out precious daylight and fresh air. Closed hatches didn't keep out the ocean, though. In the worst of storms, sea water sluiced down into steerage and sloshed back and forth underfoot, as the ship rolled with the waves. It wouldn't take long for sanitation to crowd out all other concerns. If a storm went on for a day—and sometimes a day *and* a night—the stench would be stifling. When the "All clear!" was sounded and the hatches opened, John and the other men headed up the steps to empty pans and pails used as chamber pots. Thankfully, storms were the exception.

* * *

The rising tide of immigrants to America and concern about the filthy conditions of travel prompted Congress to pass the Steerage Act of 1819, making the trip across the Atlantic safer, if no less difficult. Almost as an afterthought, the Act included a provision requiring every ship captain to file a passenger manifest with the local customs collector, who forwarded it to the Secretary of State. The passenger manifest from the St. Lawrence is the first confirmation that John and Jean had nine children. It also provides a peek into life in the cramped quarters of steerage.

Seventy-one year old John Bennet was the oldest passenger. The youngest was a two-month-old infant born to Bryan Clark and his wife. Clark was a miner, one of several American passengers returning from Europe. John Thorpe was a sixty-five-year-old farmer who also gave America as his home country. Interestingly, he was not the only Thorpe aboard. Thomas and Mary Thorpe, plus their three children, claimed England as home. Most likely, old man Thorpe had been successful in America and wanted to share that success with his son and daughter-in-law.

John Borrowman gave his occupation as farmer, as did nearly two-thirds of the men aboard the St. Lawrence. Father and son, Hugh and William McGinniss were listed as bootmakers. On the other hand, Samuel Boot was a weaver. Twenty-five-year-old Judith Connor gave her profession as dairymaid. Connor was one of only two women who were traveling alone. The other was Catherine Corcoran, a twenty-two-year-old seamstress.

Four lucky passengers occupied cabins aboard the St. Lawrence and enjoyed privacy even if they couldn't entirely escape the noise and odor from steerage below. They were

Immigrant

John Molinax, from England; William Edwards, a captain in the U.S. military who was returning home to America, and Dr. and Mrs. J. M. Gibson. The sole connection between the Gibsons in their private cabin and the Borrowmans down in steerage was that they were the only passengers from Scotland.

John and his family fell into a cautious routine with people who would be their intimate shipmates for the next month. After that, never to be seen again. One routine was imposed by the captain of every ship like the St. Lawrence.

Cramped quarters in steerage

The men and boys would be rousted on deck at consistent intervals, daily or maybe every other day, leaving more privacy in steerage for the women and girls.

John and Jean's nine children made them the largest family in steerage. Thomas Parker and his wife were next largest with seven children. Half the children in steerage were under the age of eight. In all, there were fifty-three kids within shouting distance of each other, though shouting was undoubtedly frowned upon in the interest of everyone's sanity.

Tempers could flare and drive wedges between passengers in the close confines of steerage in the St. Lawrence. But nothing pulled everyone together like the burial at sea of one-year-old William Calwell. In the terrible conditions aboard the St. Lawrence, it's a miracle there weren't more deaths. But everyone knew one was too many.

* * *

One Man's Pursuit of the American Dream

It was common knowledge among the passengers who boarded the St. Lawrence in Liverpool that an Atlantic crossing took about four weeks. But Captain Oliver Brown had made the trip enough times to know better than to promise *exactly* how long it would take. Nevertheless, by the fourth week John Borrowman was already thinking, and probably worrying, about the next leg of his family's journey beyond New York to Cincinnati, Ohio.

While the passengers were eager to reach New York, the crew was just as ready to sail on. They were paid only when the ship was under sail. More days of sailing meant more money in their pockets. Fortunately for the passengers, Captain Brown was being paid by the trip. It would end as soon as he could arrange it. He steered the St. Lawrence through The Narrows into New York harbor and in the direction of the forest of masts visible three miles ahead. He ordered the sails lowered so that he could carefully guide the ship to the dock.

There was no immigration processing—no officials brandishing papers to be stamped and signed. Ships would simply tie up near South Street at the southern end of Manhattan Island to empty themselves of their human cargo. That's where John and his family stepped off the St. Lawrence on Wednesday, May 23, 1838. It might be the ultimate irony that on the very day John arrived with a dream to own land in America, President Martin Van Buren was sending General Winfield Scott to South Carolina with orders to roust the Cherokee from land they had lived on for centuries.

* * *

Now that they were in America, the Borrowmans headed for Cincinnati. The best route to Cincinnati was down the Ohio River from Pittsburgh. From their starting point in New York, then, John would have aimed his family west toward Pittsburgh. Their first step was crossing the Hudson River.

Immigrant

John and his family walked the mile and a half west from the docks at South Street to the Hudson River ferry landing. The sights, sounds, and smells of New York were a welcome change for John and his family after the weeks spent cramped in the hold of the St. Lawrence. After doubling its population in the last decade, New York was half again the size of Liverpool, the city they had said goodbye to barely a month earlier.

Ferries had been shuttling passengers across the Hudson into New Jersey since the 1660s when Manhattan was controlled by the Dutch and still known as New Amsterdam. The Borrowmans were most likely carried on a boat owned by the Hoboken Ferry Company, which had the lion's share of the river-crossing business in 1838.

The short trip from New York to New Jersey was the first of many times John would have to dig into the cash he carried. He avoided expenses whenever he could. Boats and trains were options for west-bound travelers fortunate enough to afford them. Four years earlier, in 1834, Pennsylvania had opened a statewide combination of rail lines and canals that were known as the Main Line of Public Works.

But with a family of eleven, John had to choose a less expensive route, one that likely took them southwest to Harrisburg. From there they probably connected with what was originally built as the Forbes Road and later renamed the Pennsylvania Road. (That track is more or less the route of modern-day Highway 30 west-northwest from Harrisburg to Pittsburgh.) John's large family hitched a ride when they could and walked when they couldn't. **(Map 5)**

* * *

From Pittsburgh, the Ohio River flows a little over 450 miles along the southern border of its namesake state. In 1838, the largest city on that river was Cincinnati, known years later as the "Queen City of the West." Every boat stopped there, including the one carrying John and his family.

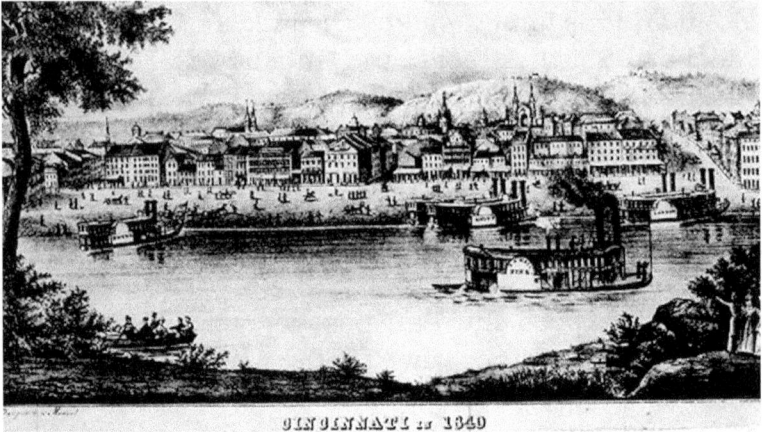

Cincinnati waterfront in 1840

Just as the river brought people to Cincinnati, it also brought livestock. By the time John arrived, the city's population had swollen to about 46,000, and it was becoming a meatpacking center. Fat and oil—by-products of meatpacking—became raw materials for other businesses making soap and candles. An English soap-maker named William Procter and an Irish candle-maker named James Gamble were competing for those raw materials, even while they were married to sisters. It was the sisters' father, Alexander Norris, who suggested a joint venture. Procter & Gamble was in its first year of business when John and his family landed.

As he stepped ashore in Cincinnati, John pulled out the crumpled piece of paper to read again the name of the man he needed to find: Peter Gibson. Gibson was a plumber at a time when plumbers were in high demand among the newly wealthy wanting the latest fashion of gas lighting installed in their homes. But, Gibson was important to John for a different reason. Peter Gibson happened to be the brother of William Gibson, who was married to Helen Ormiston, the distant relative of John's wife, Jean Ormiston. (William Gibson and Helen Ormiston were the couple that Jean had lived with many years earlier in Newlands Parish in Scotland.)

Immigrant

When John and his family left Cincinnati, the fourth son, fourteen-year-old Thomas, stayed behind as an apprentice to Peter Gibson. Is this a clue to understanding how John and Jean paid for their trip to America with only ploughman's wages? Did financial help come from the Gibsons with the expectation that a son would be apprenticed to Peter Gibson once they arrived? It is an intriguing possibility that cannot be ignored.

PETER GIBSON,
PUMP, HYDRANT AND LEAD PIPE
MANUFACTURER,
Walnut, between Fourth and Third Streets,
CINCINNATI.

Chemical Apparatus, Lead Pipes, Water Closets, Baths, &c.

Advertisement from Cincinnati City Directory, c. 1840

* * *

Land that John was hoping to own and farm lay further west of Cincinnati. After settling the details of Thomas's apprenticeship with Peter Gibson, John and the rest of the family headed for St. Louis. They continued down the Ohio River to where it met the Mississippi River at Cairo, Illinois. From there they traveled 175 miles up the Mississippi to St. Louis. By the time John and his family arrived, the city had grown far beyond its early days as a fur trading center. The advent of steamboats had helped diversify the city's economy, and St. Louis had become a jumping-off point for explorers, trappers, and would-be farmers who stocked up on supplies before heading further west.

St. Louis waterfront, c. 1840

Before they even left Scotland, John and Jean must have talked about his need to find work as soon as possible after they reached St. Louis. John realized farm work was what he did best and that he would be more valuable as a hired hand if he could take one or two sons with him. Even so, he had no idea how quickly he could find a job or what conditions he would face when he did. John and Jean had long ago realized that the whole family could not go with him when he left St. Louis to look for work.

From the advice John heard, he decided to go north from St. Louis into Illinois, where—it was said—he might find work and someday own a farm. It appears that in their planning, he and Jean had made practical decisions about who would go with him and who would stay behind. When John left, the four oldest boys—Andrew, 18, Robert, 17, Hugh, 15, and David, 13—stayed in St. Louis to find work. Their income would take care of their mother, their sister Agnes, 10, and the youngest boys, George and Adam, 5 and 4. John was the only son who went north with his father. At

Immigrant

11 years old, he was more valuable helping on a farm than he would be back in St. Louis.

John and Jean had brought their family four thousand miles from their home in Scotland. They knew the day would come when they would have to see it divided. Now that the moment was here, the pain of goodbye was masked by vows to be together again. But that would happen only for some of them.

Farmer

It was summer 1849. A quarter-section of land in Belleview Precinct, Calhoun County, Illinois—one hundred sixty acres—belonged to John Borrowman. Plowing his own farm had been the dream that brought him to America. The story of how it happened is one of hard work, sacrifice, and a little luck.

Stand on John's land on a sunny summer day today, and you will see fences separating fields of waist-high corn, bushy dark green soybeans, and alfalfa waiting to be cut and baled. When John first saw it, there was only timber and tall prairie grass. This land was frontier as recently as the turn of the 19th century when farms like John's were only beginning to tame the earth.

Surveying from the center of John's quarter section, the land rises gently from the south and continues upward past the northern horizon. To the east, the land slopes downhill at a steep angle. Rain from centuries of storms etched a pair of creases—one pointing northeast, the other southeast. These gullies are the westernmost edge of the watershed that drains into the Illinois River about five miles to the east.

The view west to the horizon is gently rolling. Just over the horizon, though, the land begins its descent to the bottom lands of the Mississippi River that snakes along about eight miles from John's farm. Other farms would start up around John's, and the area would later be called Farmers Ridge. However, an entry in a collection of biographical sketches of early settlers says that John "was the first to turn a furrow" in that part of Calhoun County.

John had worked with plenty of cast-iron plows on Dolphinton Estate back in Scotland. Plowing the land in Illinois was different. The matted roots of grasses that thrived on the prairies for centuries kept the sod locked in place. Turning a furrow meant that John had to use a new-fangled, steel-bladed plow patented by a young blacksmith and tinkerer from Northern Illinois named Deere.

Reconstruction drawing of John Deere's first self-scouring steel plow

* * *

After getting his family settled in St. Louis, John migrated north, perhaps in late 1838 or early 1839. The first thing he had to do was find work. And if you're looking for work, you go where the people are. John headed for a settlement named Gilead, about 60 miles up the Mississippi River from St. Louis. It was the de facto center of political and financial power in Western Illinois by the time he arrived.

The settlement hadn't always been named Gilead, though. That was one of the things about the land John would now call home. Names were quickly given to places and then just as quickly changed. Gilead sat less than a half-mile from the Mississippi River and was originally called Coles Grove in honor of Edward Coles, the second governor of Illinois. It was the northernmost settlement between the two rivers and the county seat of Pike County when it was organized in 1821. Gilead also happened to be home to John Shaw, a wealthy developer, and powerful political leader.

With no other counties to block it, Pike County stretched as far north as the Wisconsin Territory, and as far east as a new and growing village named Chicago. No sooner was Pike County created than the location for Pike's seat of government became a bone of contention. Shaw wanted the government to stay in Gilead because he had invested in land there. A competing group of developers wanted it moved to a location that they controlled. The battle triggered tit-for-tat lawsuits and alleged vote-buying in the early 1820s. Shaw lost the fight in the end, and Pike's county seat was relocated about 30 miles further north of Gilead to a settlement named Atlas.

Shaw ended up on the losing side again in 1824, in the effort to draft a new state constitution that would have permitted slavery in Illinois. Although he personally supported slavery, Shaw's actions were aimed more at benefiting investors like himself by encouraging immigration to Illinois by Southern slaveholders. Frustrated by the prospects for regaining power in Pike County, Shaw led local partisans in one final political tantrum.

Drawing a line from the Mississippi River to the Illinois River at roughly 39° 24' north latitude and slicing off the southern tail of Pike County, Shaw and his followers declared an entirely new county in 1825. Not surprisingly, they named it for John C. Calhoun, candidate for President the previous year and a man already earning a reputation for thumbing his nose at the government in power. With the new county in place, Shaw probably felt a personal sense of victory that Gilead would be a county seat after all.

After organizing Calhoun County in 1825, the Calhoun County Commission awarded Levi Roberts a license to open the first tavern in Gilead. Twenty-five cents boarded your horse. Another twenty-five cents bought a meal. Six cents put you in a bed for the night. And twelve cents bought you the companionship of a half-pint of whiskey.

All of this was, of course, history by the time John Borrowman set foot in Calhoun County.

It is doubtful that Borrowman crossed paths with Shaw, who had moved about eight miles further up the Mississippi River and founded a village he named Hamburg. It is certain he met Roberts, the tavern owner who was a supporter of Shaw and a man of increasing prominence in his own right. In every village since he left New York, John noticed that the local postmaster was the best person to go to for news, information, and maybe a connection to a job. The postmaster in Gilead was Levi Roberts, who had secured the appointment in 1832 after Shaw decamped for Hamburg.

It also happened that Roberts and his wife, Martha, owned a quarter-section of land in northwest Calhoun County that could easily be worth more to them if it could be farmed. Given the circumstances, Levi Roberts could be forgiven for thinking the heavens had smiled on him when John Borrowman walked in the door looking for farm work.

For John, on the other hand, it was a job he had done all his life—hired hand. But *this* job was a step closer to farming his own land.

* * *

There are no records that confirm when John came north from St. Louis. He did, in fact, exercise a precious new right when he cast his ballot in Belleview Precinct, Calhoun County, in the 1840 presidential election. Back in Scotland, only men who owned land had the right to vote. John could vote in Illinois after he lived there a mere six months. Framers of the state constitution, adopted when Illinois entered the Union in 1818, deliberately lowered the residency requirement to attract settlers like John.

A history of Calhoun County relates that a Dr. Allen Jones, himself a relative newcomer to Belleview Precinct, put together a list of almost two dozen men who cast ballots there in the 1840 election. Jones' list was not two dozen who voted on one day. It was two dozen who showed up at the polling place between October 30 and December 1, the window for voting that year. John's name was on that list, which suggests how keen he must have been to make his voice heard in his adopted country.

The election of 1840 was the first time that candidates personally courted voters rather than let others speak for them. The Whigs had drafted William Henry Harrison as their candidate. The incumbent president, Martin Van Buren, had served four years as Jackson's vice president and enjoyed Jackson's blessing in 1836 when he ran and won the presidency on his own. Then the Panic of 1837 struck, and the depression that followed gave Harrison's campaign forces plenty of ammunition to use against Van Buren during the 1840 election campaign.

John's friends and neighbors gave Harrison 80% of the vote in Calhoun County, but Van Buren managed to carry the state of Illinois. Nationwide, however, the final tally came out in Harrison's favor. Although Harrison beat Van Buren by only 147,000 out of a total 2,400,000 votes that were cast, he won an overwhelming 234 electoral votes to an embarrassing 60 for Van Buren. One of those 234 votes was cast by an elector from Springfield, a young attorney who signed his name A. Lincoln. The following March, Harrison set the record—two hours—for the longest inaugural address by an American president. What gained him a record might have cost him his life. Unfortunately, he delivered his speech on a cold, damp, blustery day, forsaking hat, coat, and gloves. He caught pneumonia and died thirty-two days later, giving him the further distinction of serving the shortest time in office.

* * *

Although voting in the election of 1840 was important to John, other news reached him sometime that year of an event with a deeper and more emotional impact. His beloved wife, Jean Ormiston, died. There are no records to confirm either date or cause, but there is a report that Jean died in St. Louis in 1840. John's oldest son, Andrew, was still in St. Louis and most likely sent word to his father in a letter that sat at the nearest post office until sometime after Jean's death.

Would John have taken the letter home with him, or opened and read it on the spot? If he read it at the post office, would others have seen his sorrow and shared their sympathy? Death at a young age was a part of life in the mid-1800s. John had surely seen enough of it growing up in Scotland. It is difficult to gauge what his reaction might have been to losing his wife. Perhaps his feelings were tempered by his distance from St. Louis and the delay in getting the news. It could not have been an easy time for him, though. The woman who had given him nine children and followed his dream of coming to America was gone. In the midst of grieving, John's only choice was to focus on his job as hired hand on the Roberts farm.

* * *

Dolphinton Estate, where John had worked in Scotland, had been in private hands since King David started giving land to Knights in 1124. The Levi Roberts farm in Calhoun County, where John now worked, had been in private hands for only twenty-one years. **(Map 6)** All the acreage in Calhoun County became part of the public lands inventory when Illinois was made a Territory in 1809. Three years later, in 1812, Congress declared the land between the Mississippi and Illinois rivers as the Military Tract and awarded a quarter-section each to veterans of the War of 1812.

So it was that Private Enoch Little traveled all the way from his home in New Hampshire and, on October 6, 1817, walked into the General Land Office in Kaskaskia, Illinois. He handed over warrant #6122 and claimed the "Southwest Quarter of Section numbered Two (2) in Township numbered Eight (8) South of Range numbered Three, West of the Fourth Principal Meridian," the legal description of what would later be the Roberts farm.

Two months later in December 1817, Pvt. Little sold his acreage for $50. After all, he was living in New Hampshire and had no interest in 160 acres so far away. Perhaps the buyer, Charles Hutchins, would. Hutchins, it turns out, sat on his investment until he eventually bundled it with seven other quarter-sections and sold them all in 1839 for a 250% return. Even with his 1280 acres, Hutchins was small potatoes compared to the speculators who would later flock to the bounty lands of the Military Tract.

The ownership record for Pvt. Little's quarter-section twists and turns, and sometimes stops at dead ends. There is no evidence, for example, to explain how it came to be owned by Levi and Martha Roberts. Nonetheless, Calhoun County records show that in February 1841, the Roberts sold that quarter-section to a trio of buyers: Frances Bosseron, George Broomfield, and William Brown.

Who were Bosseron, Broomfield, and Brown? There is no record that they bought any other land in the area or that they were anything other than speculators. They probably saw the boom of activity in the Military Tract and thought that "buy, hold while prices rise, and then sell" would be a winning strategy. The fact that an experienced hand like John Borrowman already worked the Roberts farm might have accounted for the premium of 10 cents per acre that the trio paid. Pvt. Little's original quarter-section now fetched $175. In barely two dozen years, the value had risen 350% from the $50 that Pvt. Little received from the investor, Charles Hutchins.

The change in land ownership didn't make much difference to John. He still had a job, and he had his dream.

One Man's Pursuit of the American Dream

* * *

Barely a year after the sale, a legal scrap occurred between Bosseron and his co-investors, Broomfield, and Brown. The 1841 deed from Levi and Martha Roberts conveyed an undivided one-third interest to each of the three buyers. Bosseron's actions in June 1842 are a hint that he had put up the full purchase price based on promises from Broomfield and Brown to eventually pay their shares. It appears that they never did.

Bosseron's first step was to force his partners, Broomfield and Brown, to turn to a pair of St. Louis businessmen to guarantee their shares of the original purchase price. In a fit of pique, Bosseron next used a deed of trust to squeeze Broomfield and Brown even tighter. He made it a point to include uncommon details about the acreage, livestock, and equipment that were now part of the investment.

As if that weren't enough, Bosseron also named several creditors. The first of those creditors was John Borrowman, for $19.50 most likely owed to him as the hired hand. The final name on the list was Francis Bosseron, for $500. Naming himself for the amount of $500 can be seen as Bosseron's final, angry jab to close off any possibility Broomfield or Brown could pay their debt and ever get their hands on the land.

Did John know his name was on that list? If he did, would he have cared? It is intriguing evidence that someone, somewhere, was looking out for him. Someone had taken notice of the hard-working Scot and made sure his name was first on that list. Whether that someone was the man who drew the document, or Bosseron himself, cannot be known. In any case, it took another three years for Bosseron to become fed up with waiting for his money from Broomfield and Brown.

* * *

Farmer

By 1843, John and his son had put four years' hard work into the farm. Just as he did when he worked on the farms on Dolphinton Estate, John fell in sync with its rhythms.

Corn was planted in spring. John's seed bore no resemblance to the bulging golden kernels that fill today's grain bins. He knew it as Indian corn, which was simply what folks called it. The seeds were narrower, oddly dimpled, and showed colors of brown, red, and orange. At each year's harvest, John picked out ears that would produce the best seed corn and hung them up to dry. Later, he and his son would rub the dried ears together, loosening the kernels until they dropped into a wooden bucket. He also used seed from the previous year to plant a new crop of oats to provide feed for his horses.

Spring also meant raising pigs from litters the sows had carried over the winter. If John had been lucky enough to connect with a neighbor who had a bull, there might also be a new calf.

When corn sprouted, so did the weeds. John and his son spent nearly every day hoeing in the small cornfield. In Scotland, temperatures didn't rise much past 70 degrees all summer, but in Illinois, they were already in the 80s by June. Necks and faces exposed to the sun took on a reddish cast before turning dark brown.

July's heat brought red and black raspberries, and eventually blackberries. Patches of one or the other sprouted randomly across the land. As welcome as the berries were in an otherwise bland diet, John's priorities meant that locating and gathering the sweet fruit fell to the young John.

Fall was harvest, a time of either gladness or reckoning. Had there been enough moisture? Enough sun? Had he done everything he could to keep the weeds from choking his precious crop?

Days got shorter, and temperatures dropped until winter was at hand. It was time to gather up what manure he could from the livestock and haul it out to spread over the bent and dried stubs of cornstalks. It was also a time to clear land for more crops. Trees were felled, and the stumps were burned and hacked until they could be pulled out of the way. On some winter days, the wind and cold were so bad that working outside was impossible. John would go out only long enough to care for his stock. His remaining time was spent inside, mending clothes and sharpening tools. None of his time was spent doing nothing.

John made a point of getting to know his neighbors. He realized how important it was to know who lived down in the hollow, or over the ridge, though he rarely saw them. Neighbors were important when it came time to butcher hogs. Butchering was a cold weather activity when there were fewer flies. Hams, shoulders, and sides would be cut for smoking. Unsmoked parts were sliced, fried, slathered with lard and stuffed into whatever jars might be available. A hard day of butchering meant many days of good eating ahead.

* * *

By 1844, the land speculation that was starting when Charles Hutchins invested in Pvt. Enoch Little's quarter-section in 1817 had swollen to a frenzy. The Military Tract swarmed with buyers, some acting on their own and others representing investors from the East. On a single day, June 25, 1844, New Yorkers David Nevins and John Alstyne put together a complicated financial arrangement that gave them ownership of almost 40,000 acres of Military Tract land.

Several quarter-sections that were part of that deal were not far from John. He heard talk about the buying and selling of property during one of his visits to Belleview, a settlement about three and a half miles straight southeast of the farm where he worked. But no one who lived where John lived in Calhoun Country traveled by straight line. The best route to the river bottom, where Belleview lay, followed the streams that emerged from the hills. That's how Indians created the trails that John used. (Some of those trails have become today's paved roads.)

Belleview was where John first voted in 1840 and would have received the letter from Andrew telling him of Jean's death. It was where he went when he needed those things he couldn't make or trade for—tools like an ax head or a hoe blade to replace the one worn thin from sharpening. Trips to Belleview also broke the isolation of the life he and young John led. That's where someone would have mentioned that James Polk had been elected President in 1844. The annexation of Texas in 1845 was probably big enough news to find its way to Belleview, too.

He heard about acreage changing hands at higher and higher prices, and could well have wondered how he could ever buy the farm he dreamed of. If you didn't come to America with the money to buy land—and John didn't—you had to scrimp and save as best you could. The good news was you could save because you didn't need much cash to live on. What you couldn't make or grow, you might barter for. John would have paid cash for salt and sugar, and maybe tobacco, but little else. The bad news was there were so few things you could sell to get cash money. John had his meager wages, though his bosses missed a payday here and there. Saving enough could take a long time.

But things were about to change.

* * *

In June of 1845, Frances Bosseron, whose deed of trust gave him control of the farm where John worked, was under pressure from creditors in St. Louis. The triggering event is not clear, but the result was a sheriff's sale of the land. Records in the Calhoun County Clerk's office reveal that John Red, Calhoun County sheriff at the time, was familiar with land sales arising from judgments issued from the nearby courthouse. Red had done a little speculating on his own, buying properties that fell under the judge's hammer.

Those same records, however, show that on this particular parcel of land, on this particular sale day, John Borrowman was "the highest and best bidder therefore." John's position as the first creditor in Bosseron's deed of trust didn't give him any advantage at sale time. He still had to pay in cash. The amount isn't specified.

Though there is no record of how much John paid, it had to have been a bargain. The Scottish hired hand had his dream. Owning land was what he had come all this way to do. He had kept his head down and worked hard. In off-hand moments back at Meadowhead Farm or Roberton Mains on Dolphinton Estate, John and his co-workers talked to each other about what they would do if only they owned a farm. Now, John did.

Like any good hired hand, John always treated the farm as if it were his own. That fall he brought in the harvest and then worked through the winter at his usual chores as he had done so many seasons before. But it felt different now because the crops were his. The stock was his. The land and everything on it was *his*. Even his neighbors probably saw him a little bit differently. He was no longer just a hired hand.

* * *

The farming cycle began again in the spring of 1846. John's thoughts about what he could—and should—do with his farm became more focused. Tips for smarter farming were a common topic at Belleview. John listened a little more carefully now. Like farmers then and since, John was land-rich and cash-poor. And like any progressive farmer, he wanted to add to his livestock and put more acreage into crops. To do that, he needed cash.

Loans were very hard to come by. Banks hadn't yet opened west of the Illinois River. The nearest—still sixty miles away—was the Bank of Edwardsville, which began business around the time Illinois became a state in 1818.

Farmer

Eventually Col. William B. Ross opened a bank in Pike County. Ross was part of the same faction that had outmaneuvered John Shaw in getting the Pike County government moved from Gilead to Atlas in the early 1820s. By 1833, the Ross forces birthed a new town named after their hometown, Pittsfield, Massachusetts. They relocated the center of Pike County government there from Atlas. Ross's bank in Pittsfield, Illinois opened in 1854, too late to help John Borrowman.

In 1846, there were simply too few local people, or banks, with the resources to loan John the money he needed. He likely picked up leads from conversations he heard in Belleview. In any event, with the harvest laid in and the end of 1846 approaching, John arranged to meet with Daniel Bush, an attorney in Pittsfield. Bush was a friend of Col. Ross in Massachusetts and likely had come to his new hometown at Ross's suggestion.

The long, tiring day on horseback to Bush's office in Pittsfield provided John plenty of time to think about how he would make his case for a loan. Bush listened to John's story about coming to America, about working on the farm and the improbable way it had become his. There must have been something Bush heard in that story that inspired him to take a chance on the earnest farmer standing in front of him. The result was that on December 17, 1846, John mortgaged his 160 acres in a five-year note for $150 at six percent interest.

Bush would most likely have sent John on his way with a bag full of half eagles, eagles, and double eagles: $5, $10, and $20 coins. Paper money was issued only by state banks and was considered untrustworthy because it wasn't always backed by specie (coin). As he rode back to his farm, the muffled clink in his saddlebag reminded John that his future was again in the hands of another man.

In January 1847, the Calhoun County Courthouse at Gilead burned, and the government moved north to Hamburg.

Once again, rivalries erupted over where the county seat would finally be located. Hamburg wanted to keep it. Gilead wanted it back.

Meanwhile, on the east side of the county, another developer lobbied to move the seat of government to the village that bore his name. When Benjamin Childs first arrived in the area of Terry's Landing in 1835, he bought land from Dr. William Terry and proceeded to open businesses and sell lots. In time, "Childs Landing" replaced "Terry's Landing" as the name for the tiny settlement on the west bank of the Illinois River. Now Childs was offering the County Commission five acres of land and fifty thousand bricks if they would move the county seat to Childs Landing.

Just before a county-wide election to choose the location of the county seat, Childs threw a free barbecue dinner. Voters must have been persuaded by the meal, because when the ballots were counted Childs Landing had more votes than Gilead and Hamburg combined. In the spirit of the "never-say-die" John Shaw, Hamburg citizens still pleaded to keep the county seat in Hamburg. The commissioners gave their petition a dismissive wave, though, and confirmed the choice of Childs Landing. Their first official meeting there was in December 1847. When a post office was established that same year, Benjamin Childs was the obvious choice for postmaster.

* * *

The year 1848 marked John's tenth in his new country. In May, John's oldest son, Andrew, now twenty-eight, moved to Calhoun County from St. Louis. Andrew brought his wife, Sarah Hunter, whom he had married three years earlier, on August 6, 1845. Andrew and Sarah made the house more crowded, but John made good use of the couple's help on the farm. By August of 1848, John repaid the $150 he had borrowed from Daniel Bush. How did John manage to save such a sum? Perhaps he bought, raised, and sold enough livestock to earn the $150. Or maybe it was frugality—tucking away every little bit in a safe place? Could Andrew have contributed a few dollars he had saved while he and Sarah lived in St. Louis? Whatever the case, John paid his debt and reclaimed title to his land three years before payment was due.

Harvest time turned to winter, and winter turned to spring. Each year, John's steel-bladed prairie plow cleared more and more prairie grass, and now he had a farm to be proud of. Over time, the soil loosened enough so that his smaller plow easily broke it up. Still, it took every bit of two weeks slapping the reins against the backs of the mares to ready the ten acres John sowed in corn that spring of 1849.

A sack of leftover seed corn sitting under roof and waiting for next year's planting was a testimony to the thrifty Scot in him that had been so careful at planting time. Also sheltered from the ruinous rain was the prior harvest from individual plots of wheat and oats.

Each of his two mares had a colt. It might take a few years, but eventually, he would have a second team that would let him work even more acreage. Better still, if the pair he owned stayed healthy and—more importantly—had more colts, he could sell one or both a bit sooner and invest in more livestock.

John had two milk cows—one red, the other brown—that provided milk and butter for his table. There were also two steers and three heifers. Paths worn by their hooves meandered through the waist high grass toward their favorite watering holes. When the wind was right, John could smell the pigs that had rooted out a series of wallows. They usually managed to work out a spot near a stream, or where rainfall drained. He could hear them snuffling and snorting in competition for what remained of the prime spots in the mud. John had fifteen sows that were nursing twenty-two pigs, and he was counting the days until they could be weaned. Scattered around the wallows were another thirty-one hogs he was fattening for the market. With an eye on the future of his farm, he also kept a bull and a boar.

John's horses were good for pulling the plow and dragging the trees he felled to clear more land, and they made for more than adequate transport when ridden. But, when it came to moving this and that from here to there, the choice was to carry it in his cart or on his back. That made the horse-drawn cart his—and every farmer's—most prized possession.

All John's implements were built with iron and steel, including ax blades, shovels, hoes, and wheels for his cart. But for every piece of metal, there was wood that held it together. Wood rotted, and wood broke. And when it broke, the only option was to fashion a replacement from a fallen limb or tree trunk. With a pair of planes, the right augur, and a drawing knife, he managed to keep almost everything in decent repair. Like some cruel joke, though, nothing broke except when he needed it most. That meant work stopped until it was fixed.

It took about an hour to do chores every morning, and another hour in the evening. In between there was always something to do to keep the farm running.

* * *

It was now late June 1849, about a week after the summer solstice. Dawn came a few minutes later as daylight began the slow disappearing act that would finish six months later. Then the annual cycle would begin again.

On this particular dawn, John was sorting off the lighter weight hogs until he had gathered the heavier ones he would sell. For the past few weeks, he had been thinking about going to market. It was just a question of when he would make the trip. Anything he knew or thought he knew about the prices his hogs would bring was weeks—maybe months—old. John made it a point to visit Belleview to get the latest information on hog prices.

Farmer

John also heard talk in Belleview about how cholera had come to St. Louis. He remembered his feeling of fear when cholera swept through Scotland in 1832. In Dolphinton that year, Richard Mackenzie, Laird of the Dolphinton Estate, wrote to tell the Kirk Session that he had arranged for "a parcel of cholera medicines with instructions from the Board of Health." In his letter, Mackenzie promised to "get a medical man to go out from Edinburgh at an allowance of two guineas a day . . ." if it became necessary.

As bad as cholera was, John told himself on the way home from Belleview, the disease had not touched him back then. He thought about the market day ahead and convinced himself that cholera would not touch him now, either. He talked with his sons, Andrew and John, about his plan to make another trip to the hog market near St. Louis and what they needed to get done while he was gone. At twenty-nine and twenty-two, Andrew and John were an integral part of the farm operation.

* * *

John stripped a tree of one of its thinner branches and used it as a switch to gather his small herd. There is no record of how many hogs he took to market that day. There were at least five or six, but could have been as many as eight or ten. Modern day hogs are bred for their lean meat. Hogs in John's day were bred for lard, which meant they were fatter and more docile. Eight or ten would not have been beyond his ability to manage.

Snapping his switch, John drove his hogs south about a mile, then turned them east onto a trail through the underbrush. The land began to fall away where the trail started to follow a stream. Off to John's left was a timber-covered ridge. After a mile or so of the slope, John came out onto flat land. The stream he had been following merged with another that had started on the opposite side of the ridge. Together they became East Panther Creek, which meandered two and a half miles until it emptied into the Illinois River. John's destination was the steamboat landing that had started up there and was later known as Cliffdale Landing. **(Map 7)**

Steamboats had been coming this far up the Illinois for more than fifteen years and enjoyed a cooperative relationship with landowners along the river. Captains needed wood to fire their boilers. If the landowner could supply timber, the steamboat would stop. If the boat stopped, the landowner also stood to gain from the commercial potential of people who came to board. In some places, towns would grow and develop. In others, the timber would play out, and the captain would find another location to get fuel.

Cutting timber was one thing. Getting it out to the shore for the boats was another. Even a shallow waterway like East Panther Creek would make it easier to get firewood to the riverbank. John stopped along his path and sat on one of the stumps left from where timber had been cut and floated out to the steamboat landing that had developed where the creek flowed into the river. A boat would happen along soon, and he would begin the next leg of his journey.

Livestock was a common sight on an Illinois River steamboat. John drove his few hogs on board and herded them together to one side. The sound from the cattle elsewhere on the deck was familiar

The Ben Campbell loaded with livestock

to John's hogs. The steamboat whistle was *not*. The first blast startled them and sent their ears shooting skyward. After that, they paid little attention.

Farmer

John kept an eye on his hogs and exchanged hellos with other farmers watching their own stock. He was interested in what they could tell him about prices, of course, but it didn't matter now. He was on his way and would take whatever the market offered. Here and there were murmurings about cholera. According to some of the voices that John heard, cholera was divine retribution—God's justice on the thoughtless and immoral. He could hardly put himself in that category.

Almost an hour downstream was Crader's Landing, where a fueling stop had developed on the western shore. The landing was a little downstream from the north end of Hurricane Island. Captains pulling away from shore had to maneuver back upstream and around to the east side of the island to catch the river channel.

Six miles further downriver, the recently renamed Calhoun County seat of Hardin was a reminder of the much-debated Mexican War, which had ended only a year earlier. Hardin had been Childs Landing but got its new name to honor Col. John Hardin, who was killed at the Battle of Buena Vista in Mexico. Hardin was the Congressman from the 7th District of Illinois, which included Calhoun County, and had defeated Abraham Lincoln for the seat. Over on the shore, John saw evidence that the county government was settling in for business. The courthouse had been finished the previous year, and bids sent out to construct a jail. South of the courthouse was Andrew Uhrig's store and saloon. Uhrig had lent a hand to Childs' effort to lure the government to the east side of the county. Now he was reaping the benefits.

The Illinois joined with the Mississippi another twenty miles downriver, and the boat responded to the change in current. John looked to his left and saw the little town of Grafton. Further on was Alton, sited just upstream from where the Missouri River joined the mighty Mississippi. A dozen or so more miles downriver from Alton, the steamboat nosed into the shore on the Illinois side of the river, and John got his hogs stirring. They had finally quieted on the trip downriver but were again nervously grunting and snuffling. John herded them down the gangplank toward the market at Paps Town. **(Map 8)**

Paps Town was where livestock buyers gathered, ready to trade cold, hard cash for bacon, ham, and lard on the hoof. The tiny village was absorbed into East St. Louis, Illinois, in 1859. Livestock buyers continued to come in numbers that attracted the attention of East Coast venture capitalists, who built the National Stockyards there in 1873.

John drove his hogs along a muddy trail in search of a buyer whom he remembered from one of his previous trips. Back in Dolphinton, people came out for market days only twice a year, Martinmas and Whitsunday. In Paps Town, every day was market day, and there were plenty of people for John to meet and talk with. In every settlement like Paps Town, taverns opened to feed and water the people. Churches opened to save their souls. John didn't take time for either.

John found his buyer and, pushing his hogs one at a time onto the scale, anxiously waited to learn what his hard work was going to draw out of the buyer's pocket. John already had plans for some of that money. Someone in the household always needed shoes or clothes. The horses needed a larger shelter, and that project required nails. Shoes, clothes, and nails—all required cash.

It's hard to imagine that cholera was not part of the conversation between John and the hog buyer. That month's death toll for St. Louis was already inching past six hundred. The devastating disease had spread across the United States, following the flow of immigration. No one realized that cholera flourished wherever water supplies were contaminated by sewage. That included places like St. Louis and, just a ferry ride across the Mississippi River, Paps Town in Illinois.

Farmer

Cholera victims were easy to spot. Bouts of diarrhea alternated with spasmodic retching. Their skin turned blue and was drawn and pinched from the severe dehydration. Onset could be sudden, causing them to simply pitch over in the street. Those who were struck in the morning were often dead by nightfall. Those who caught the disease in the evening rarely lived to see the next day.

Whether or not John had contact with any victims, he could not have missed hearing enough about the disease to make him want to escape quickly from this place and get back to his farm and his family. Carefully guarding his cash, John made his way to where he could catch a steamboat headed upriver to the landing at East Panther Creek. He found one, paid his fare, and hurried aboard. Though he was curious what other passengers had heard about cholera, his good sense—or fear—led him to keep to himself.

The steamboat reversed its big paddlewheel long enough to pull out into the channel where it faced the current. With a blast of the whistle, the paddlewheel changed direction and began pushing the steamboat upriver. John drew a deep, slow breath. *Surely the steamboat captain wouldn't have let anyone on board who had cholera.* He let that thought relieve him of worry.

* * *

The boat continued its labored journey north. Soon enough it passed the mouth of the Missouri River on the west bank, then drew abreast of Alton on the east. John quietly counted the money from selling his hogs and thought about his sons. They worked tirelessly. Like all fathers, he wanted their lives to be better than his. On his next visit to Belleview, he would look for some way he could reward them.

Deep in thoughts of his family, John was interrupted by a commotion from the other side of the boat. He thought he heard mention of cholera followed by demands being shouted at the captain. Once on board, though, John had kept to himself. No need to get involved.

Chuffing against the current, the steamboat drew closer to Grafton and maneuvered starboard into the mouth of the Illinois River. John knew he was almost halfway home.

The previous commotion died away only when a frail and sickly man had been quarantined to a spot away from other passengers. Out of the corner of his eye, John could see the man shivering. Because it wasn't understood what caused cholera or where the disease came from, anyone suspected of being a victim was shunned. No one wanted to take any chances. Not until years later did it become known that cholera lurked in the mud and the slop like that of Paps Town back downstream, or that direct human contact had little to do with it.

It was when he had the village of Hardin in sight about two hours from his destination that John tasted the salt of sweat on his lips and felt his body warming. He knew what it was like to soak a shirt with sweat as he walked behind his team of mares plowing in the hot sun. This was something else. He gripped the rail to steady himself. By the time the boat reached Hurricane Island, John's leg muscles had tightened in spasms that made him lurch. He gripped the rail until his knuckles turned white. His stomach clenched, and it was only by sheer force of will that he kept his mid-day meal down.

As the steamboat drew closer to the landing at East Panther Creek, John managed to pull himself near to where he could step quickly onto the gangplank and avoid the stares of other passengers. The boat nosed into the bank, the ramp was lowered, and John stumbled onto the shore. Barely a dozen steps further on, the bitterness he had managed to suppress on the boat came dribbling out of his lips and onto his shirt. In the same moment, a foul mix of liquid and solid soiled his pants. John could no longer deny that cholera had invaded his body. He felt again for the money. He wanted to hand it to his sons and tell them it was for their future on the farm.

John staggered along the south bank of East Panther Creek, feeling his strength leaving him. He looked up ahead where the streams split, and beyond that to where he would begin the climb through the brush and timber up to his farm. He worried that even if his body obliged, carrying the money home meant delivering cholera to his family. He faced a terrible choice.

A moment later John was veering off to the left of the stream, looking for shelter in a rough log corncrib he had seen on a previous trip. (The corncrib was in a secluded valley that, eighty or so years later, would be known as Drag Out Hollow. **Map 9**) Falling, rising, and then falling again, John stumbled to the door of the corncrib. He crawled inside and dragged himself over to one corner. His body shuddered from the cramps that came quickly and severely. His breathing became labored, more shallow, and then stopped altogether.

* * *

John had been in America nearly a dozen years. He had traveled an ocean and then half a continent to plow his own farm. And with the sort of good fortune that his friends on Dolphinton Estate would never have believed, he became a farmer.

John's dream lasted only four years. Finding his way to that dream meant saying goodbye to nearly all his family. In the end, passing that dream on to his sons cost him his own life.

Were those four short years worth the price he paid? There is only one answer for a dreamer like John.

Epilogue

Brothers Andrew and John Borrowman found their father's body within a day or two of his death and arranged for his burial in what is known as Smith Cemetery. The cemetery is in a small clearing on a hillside across the valley from Drag Out Hollow, where John Borrowman died in the corn crib. John's burial plot is likely marked by one of the stubs of rock protruding from the ground. Though it is hidden by trees and brush, the cemetery can be located by turning south from East Panther Creek Road approximately three miles east of Illinois Hwy 100. The gravel road crosses a shallow creek bed and curves to the right around the base of the hill (GPS coordinates: 39° 21' 59" - 90° 40' 34").

John's estate (including tools, equipment, and livestock, but not the farm itself) was appraised on August 23, 1849, at $396.01. An auction held a day later generated $493.03 in sales. As individual and joint buyers, Andrew and John themselves accounted for $306.93 of that amount. Were they actually the highest bidders for all those items? Or, did sympathetic neighbors hold back on their offers? The more we learn, the more questions we have.

Research while writing this book also provides a clearer picture of the lives of each of John's children—the next generation.

Andrew (b. February 24, 1820; d. January 6, 1885) After his father died, Andrew continued to live and work on the farm he and his brother, John, jointly inherited from their father. Andrew and his wife Sarah eventually accumulated 400 acres. During the Civil War, Andrew served with Company F of the 28th (Consolidated) Infantry Regiment. He was 44 when he mustered on September 27, 1864, leaving his wife, children, and farm behind. With Lee's surrender only six and a half months away, it's a safe bet that Andrew served because he was drafted. He and Sarah had eight children, two of whom died in infancy. He died a little more than a month shy of his sixty-sixth birthday and is buried in McConnell Cemetery in Calhoun County.

Robert (b. April 1, 1821; d. unknown) Absent evidence to the contrary, it is fair to assume that Robert made it to St. Louis with the rest of the family. No records have been found that definitively reveal what happened to him, however. An R. D. Barrowman was buried in Bellefontaine Cemetery in St. Louis in August 1894. Even allowing for misspelling, there is no way to confirm that R. D. is Robert.

Hugh (b. September 12, 1822; d. February 1849) Hugh was the oldest of the family still living in St. Louis after Andrew moved to Calhoun County in 1846. Early in 1849, Hugh, only 27, contracted a serious illness. Records are not clear about the diagnosis. It was severe enough, however, that he wrote a will on January 20, 1849. He died in early February, but his burial place is unknown. Records tell us that Freeman Little handled the funeral arrangements, charging $12.50 for a coffin and case, and another $5.00 for a "fine shroud."

Thomas (b. January 9, 1824; d. November 23, 1908) Thomas worked for Peter Gibson for about twelve years, including his original apprenticeship immediately after arriving in America. Then he opened his own plumbing business and ran it successfully for another ten years. Thomas went to Olney, Illinois, in 1859 and took up farming. In 1867, he moved to Vincennes, Indiana, where he opened a meatpacking business and later became a successful grain merchant. He and his wife, Isabella, had nine children. He died at the age of 84 and is buried in Vincennes.

Epilogue

David (b. August 8, 1825; d. January 7, 1909) David left St. Louis sometime before Hugh died, and moved to Nashville, Tennessee, to learn to be a stonecutter. The 1850 federal census places him there. In 1854, he married Jane Barker in Nashville. They moved to Hannibal, Missouri, in 1855 and then to Griggsville, Illinois, in March 1866. David and Jane had five children, three of whom died in infancy. Cemetery monuments throughout the area are a silent testimony to his skills as a stonecutter. David died at the age of 83 and is buried in Griggsville.

John (b. March 16, 1827; d. March 7, 1892) John, the son who left St. Louis with his father, worked with Andrew to farm their father's quarter-section in Belleview Precinct, in Calhoun County. He lived with Andrew and Sarah until he married Julianne Harpole in February 1857. After Julianne died in 1858, John married Sarah Ball, and they had six children. John was the first of the family to buy land in Pike County. John died at the age of 65 and is buried in McConnell Cemetery in Calhoun County.

Agnes (b. July 8, 1829; d. 1846) Agnes, John's only daughter, left St. Louis to go to Cincinnati after her mother died in 1840. Agnes was eleven years old—twelve at most—and surrounded by brothers. She most likely went to live with William Gibson and Helen Ormiston (remember *them*?), who came to America in 1840 to be near William's brother, Peter Gibson, in Cincinnati. Some years later, Agnes's brother Thomas (who was still living there at the time) reported that Agnes died in Cincinnati in 1846—the cause of death is unknown.

George (b. circa 1833; d. April 1873) Once his family arrived in St. Louis, George grew up there and never left. Civil War Draft Registration Records for St. Louis County indicate he was married, though nothing has been found about his wife. George worked as a clerk in the post office for many years. His reliable, civil service employment might account for the fact that his estate was just over $1600 (roughly $400,000 today). George is buried in the Calvary Catholic Cemetery in St. Louis.

Adam (b. circa 1835; d. unknown) Adam, the youngest, moved to Cincinnati together with his sister Agnes sometime around 1840. He was barely six and likely needed more looking after than his brothers could provide. According to a report from Thomas (the same report that referenced Agnes' death), Adam lived with Thomas in 1850 and 1851. Thomas's report also says that Adam left Cincinnati in 1851 in the company of friends, headed for the goldfields of California. Adam was never heard from, and his brothers presumed him dead. According to the 1870 Federal Census, however, Adam was working for the Placer Mining Company in Pioneerville, in the Idaho Territory. Ten years later, the 1880 federal census listed him as a farmer in Missoula, Montana. After that, Adam no longer appears in any records.

* * *

Today, in John's homeland of Scotland, the quiet village of Dolphinton straddles the A702, the two-lane highway that connects Edinburgh with Biggar. Dolphinton would be considered the proverbial "wide spot in the road." Owing to cost constraints, the Dolphinton, Dunsyre, Elsrickle, and Walston Parishes have been combined into Black Mount Parish. Rev. Mike Fucella officiates at Sunday services still held in the original Dolphinton Parish Church.

In the mid-1980s, the 2300-acre Dolphinton Estate was broken up into six individual farms, miscellaneous pasture and woodlands, and a sand and gravel quarry, all of which were put up for sale. Roberton Mains continues to be an active sheep farm. The barn at Meadowhead Farm where John Borrowman worked has been renovated into a comfortable, self-catering cottage available for rent by the week.

Epilogue

Angela Mackenzie, the great-great-great granddaughter of Richard Mackenzie, Laird of the estate when John worked there as a hired hand, owns and manages a farm located at the north edge of Dolphinton.

Nowhere, perhaps, has time brought more change than on the quarter-section of land that John owned in Calhoun County. When John worked there for Levi Roberts in 1841, Roberts sold the land for about $1.10 an acre. Today, acreage within that same quarter-section is valued at $2,125 an acre.

Although John's dream of plowing his own farm lasted only four years, his legacy as a successful farmer continues. John's farm in Calhoun County was a mere 160 acres. Nearly 170 years and six generations later, his direct Borrowman descendants in Pike County, Illinois, own over 15,000 acres of farmland, conservatively valued at $75,000,000.

Maps

Map 1

Dolphinton, Scotland

Map 2

Dolphinton and surrounding parishes

Dunsyre, Dolphinton, Walston, and Biggar parishes are in Lanarkshire.

West Linton, Newlands, Kirkurd, Skirling, and Broughton parishes are in Peebleshire.

Map 3

Counties in southern Scotland

John and Jean Ormiston were born at Morham Parish in East Lothian, about 47 miles east of Dolphinton Parish.

Map 4

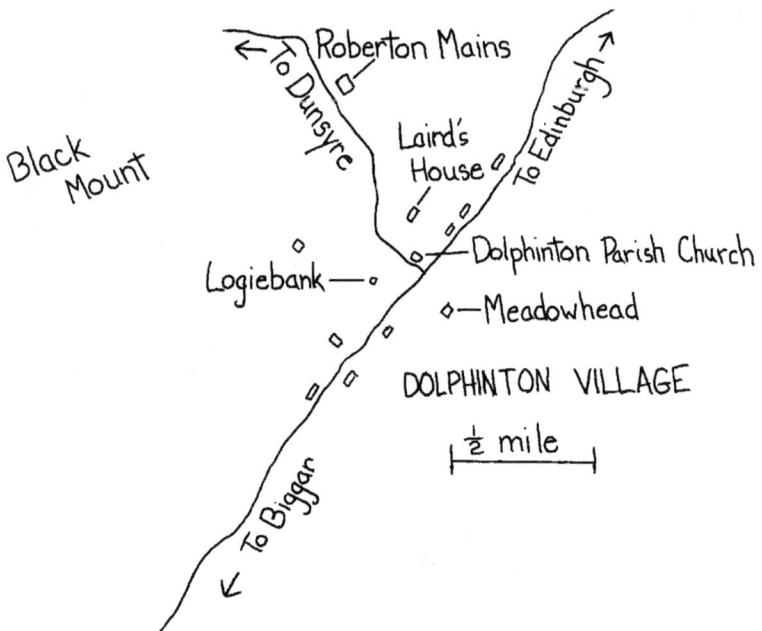

Black Mount

To Dunsyre →

Roberton Mains

Laird's House

To Edinburgh ↗

Logiebank — ○

○ — Dolphinton Parish Church

◇ — Meadowhead

DOLPHINTON VILLAGE

$\frac{1}{2}$ mile

← To Biggar

Dolphinton Village

Map 5

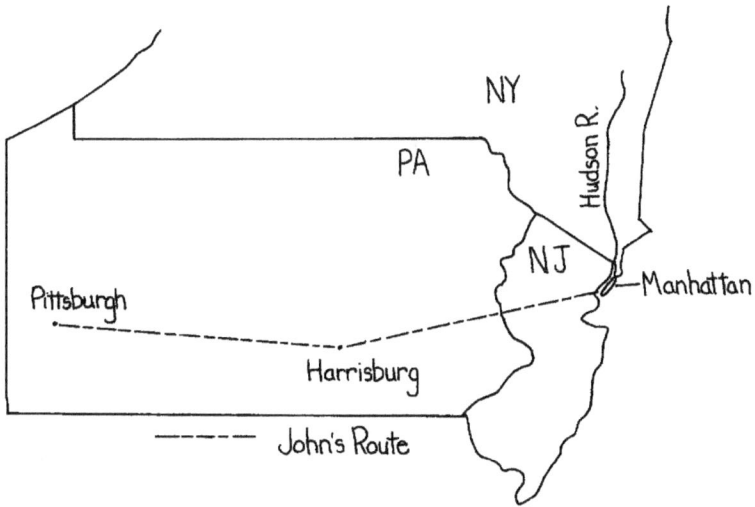

NY

PA

Hudson R.

NJ

Pittsburgh

Manhattan

Harrisburg

------ John's Route

**John's likely route from New York City
to the Ohio River at Pittsburgh**

Map 6

Belleview

Levi Roberts
Farm

Missouri

Illinois

Hamburg

Gilead
(Coles Grove)

Illinois R.

Mississippi R.

Mississippi R.

Missouri R.

St. Louis

Settlements along the Mississippi River

Map 7

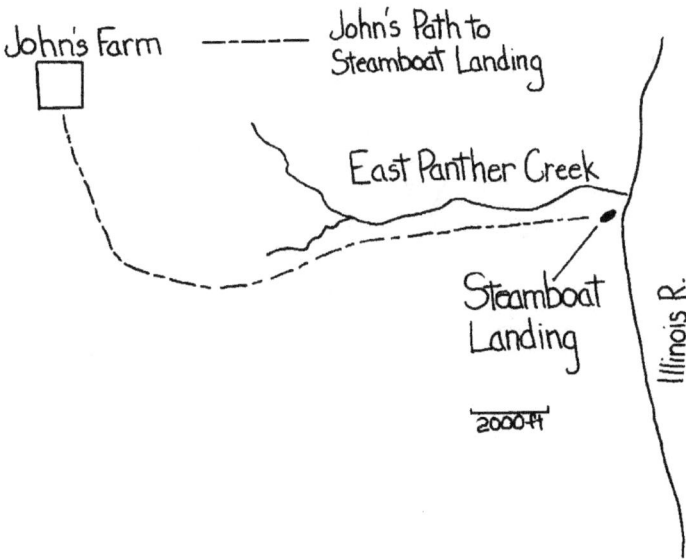

John's Farm   — — — —   John's Path to
Steamboat Landing

East Panther Creek

Steamboat
Landing

Illinois R.

2000 ft

John's path to the steamboat landing

Map 8

Steamboat Landing
East Panther Creek
Illinois
Missouri
Crader's Landing
Hardin (Childs Landing)
Mississippi R.
Illinois R.
Grafton
Mississippi R.
Alton
Missouri R.
Paps Town

**Route of John's steamboat from
East Panther Creek to market at Paps Town**

Map 9

John's Farm ------- John's Path from Steamboat Landing

Smith Cemetery

East Panther Creek

Steamboat Landing

Illinois R.

Corncrib

2000 ft

Drag Out Hollow

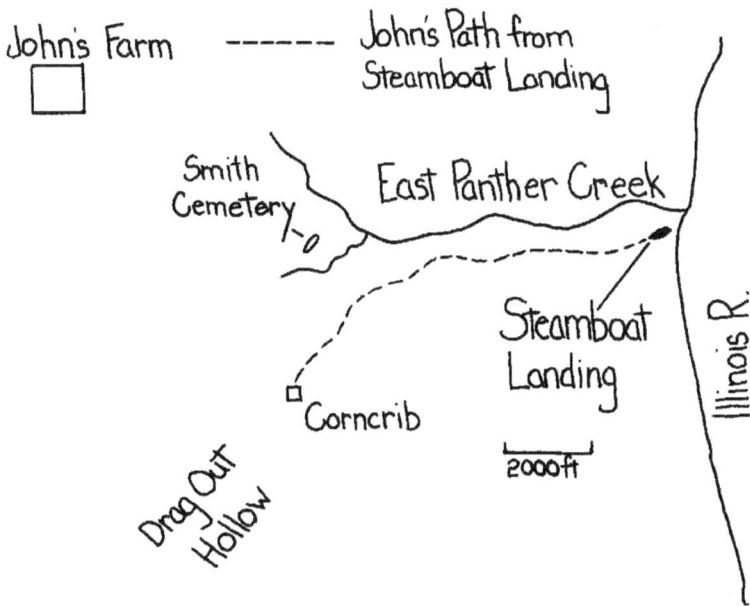

John's path from the steamboat landing to his death in the corncrib

Source Documents

Research for this book occurred over several years and uncovered many documents. Some were directly related to John's story but in too poor of a condition to be included in this book. Others were of good quality and fascinating in their subject matter, though less relevant to John's life.

Source Document 4 is the source for the detailed description of John's farm included in Chapter 3.

Source Document 6 was an exceptional, last-minute find. I encourage readers to give it special attention. It is barely legible, so I have transcribed the entire document for convenient reading.

The documents that follow give the reader a closer look at the life of this ploughman, immigrant, and farmer.

Source Document 1
Meadowhead Farm in 1827

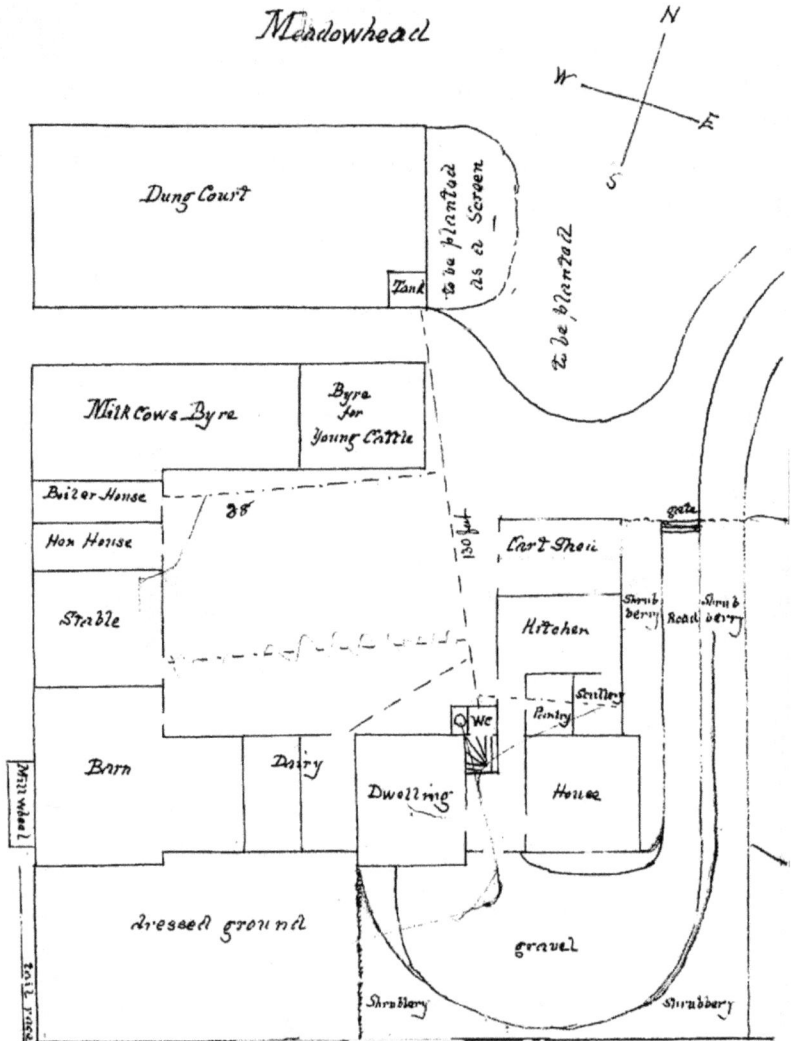

Meadowhead

N
W
E
S

Dung Court

to be planted as a Screen

to be Planted

Tank

Milk Cows Byre

Byre for Young Cattle

Builer House

38

Hen House

130 feet

Cart Shed

gate

Stable

Kitchen

Shrubbery   Road   Shrubbery

WC

Scullery

Pantry

Millwheel

Barn

Dairy

Dwelling

House

toll race

dressed ground

gravel

Shrubbery

Shrubbery

This is what Meadowhead Farm looked like
when John worked there. The sketch is from the
Mackenzie (Dolphinton) Estate Archives held at the
Mitchell Library in Glasgow.

Source Document 2
Excerpt from the records of
Dolphinton Parish Kirk Session

On September 23, 1825, the day after the baptism of his fourth son David, John paid two shillings, sixpence as a "baptism fee." No records of baptism fees for John's other children exist. This record was found at Register House, Edinburgh.

Source Document 3
St. Lawrence passenger manifest, excerpted

Report of passengers on board the ship St. Lawrence at New York,
Oliver Brown, Master from Liverpool to New York
Cabin Passengers
37 Dr. J.M. Gibson, Scotland 33 Capt. William Edwards New York
40 Mrs. Mary "   "   29 Mr. John Hardiman Mulinax England
Steerage Passengers

The Steerage Act of 1819 required every ship captain to file a
passenger list with the local customs house. Occupation is
listed, as are ages (see numbers). This document is the
first confirmation that John and Jean "Burman" had
nine children. It wouldn't be the last time the
Borrowman family name was misspelled.

Source Document 4
Excerpt from the official record of John's estate sale

Transcript of top paragraph: "List of sales of the goods and chattels of the estate of John Borrowman, late of Calhoun County, deceased, sold at public auction by the undersigned administrator of said estate on the 24th day of August, 1849."

Source Document 5
Advertisement for Military Tract

This advertisement for the "Bounty Lands" of the Military
Tract might have prompted Pvt. Enoch Little to travel
to Kaskaskia to claim his quarter-section. Pvt. Little's
160 acres eventually became John's farm.

Source Document 6
Affidavit of Thomas Borrowman

State of Missouri
County of St. Louis

Personally appeared before me, George H. Shields, a notary public in and for said County, qualified 23 January 1874, for a term to expire 21st January 1878, on this twentieth day of July A.D. eighteen hundred and seventy five, Thomas Borrowman, of lawful age, who being by me duly sworn, on his oath says, that he is a resident of the City of Vincennes in Knox County, State of Indiana, and that he is a brother to the late George R. Borrowman who died at the City of St. Louis State of Missouri on or about the 15th day of April 1873, that the parents of said George R. Borrowman died many years ago, and that said George R. Borrowman had one sister who died in 1846 at Cincinnati, Ohio, without issue, and five brothers, viz: 1st Andrew Borrowman who now resides in Calhoun County, Illinois, 2nd Thomas Borrowman, this affiant, 3rd David Borrowman of Griggsville, Pike County, Illinois, 4th John Borrowman, who resides in Calhoun County, Illinois, and 5th Adam Borrowman who resided with this affiant in Cincinnati, Ohio, and left that city, as near as this affiant can recollect, in the early part of summer of 1851, in company with other persons on a journey to the Territory (now State) of California, and no tidings of the whereabouts of said Adam Borrowman have ever come to this affiant since said Adam Borrowman left the City of Cincinnati in eighteen hundred and fifty one, and that said Adam at the time when he left Cincinnati as aforesaid, was about fifteen or sixteen years old and single, and that all the brothers have believed him and still believe him said Adam Borrowman to be dead, and that therefore to the best of this affiant's knowledge and belief the above named Andrew Borrowman, Thomas Borrowman, David Borrowman and John Borrowman are the only surviving brothers and next of kin of said George R. Borrowman deceased and that each of them is over twenty one years old; and further deponent says not.

Thos. Borrowman

Sworn to and subscribed before me
this 20th day of July A.D. 1875.
George H. Shields

Thomas Borrowman (living in Vincennes at the time) swore this affidavit in connection with the probate of the estate of his brother George. The affidavit reveals heretofore unknown details about Adam and Agnes.

Source Document 6 (cont.)
Transcription of affidavit
of Thomas Borrowman

State of Missouri
County of St. Louis

Personally appeared before me, George H. Skiller, a Notary Public in and for said County, qualified 23rd January 1874, for a term to expire 21st January 1878, on this twentieth day of July AD, Eighteen Hundred and Seventy-five, Thomas Borrowman, of lawful age, who being by me duly sworn on his oath says, that he is a resident of the City of Vincennes, in Knox County, State of Indiana, and that he is a brother to the late George R. Borrowman, who died at the City of St. Louis, State of Missouri on or about the 15th day of April 1873, that the parents of said George R. Borrowman died many years ago, and that said George R. Borrowman had one sister who died in 1846 at Cincinnati, Ohio, without issue, and five brothers, viz: 1st Andrew Borrowman, who now resides in Calhoun County, Illinois, 2nd Thomas Borrowman, this affiant, 3rd David Borrowman of Griggsville, Pike County, Illinois, 4th John Borrowman, who resides in Calhoun County, Illinois and 5th Adam Borrowman who resided with this affiant in Cincinnati, Ohio in 1850 & 1851, and left that city, as near as this affiant can recollect, in the early part of the summer of 1851, in company with other persons on a journey to the Territory (now State) of California, and no tidings of the whereabouts of said Adam Borrowman have ever come to this affiant since said Adam Borrowman left the City of Cincinnati in eighteen hundred and fifty one, and that said Adam at the time when he left Cincinnati, as aforesaid, was about fifteen or sixteen years old and single, and that all the brothers have believed him

Source Document 6 (cont.)

and still believe him, said Adam Borrowman to be dead, and that therefore to the best of this affiant's knowledge and belief the above named Andrew Borrowman, Thomas Borrowman, David Borrowman and John Borrowman are the only surviving brothers, and next of kin of said George R. Borrowman deceased and that each of them is over twenty one years old; and further deponent says not.

(Signed) Thos Borrowman

Sworn to and subscribed before me
this 20th day of July A.D. 1875

George H. Skiller, Notary Public

Bibliography

Belich, James. *Replenishing the Earth: The Settler Revolution and the Rise of the Anglo-World, 1783-1939.* New York: Oxford University Press, 2009.

Borrowman, David S., and Fern Borrowman. *Borrowman Family Heritage.* Published by authors, 1980.

Brown, Callum. *Religion and Society in Scotland since 1717.* Edinburgh: Edinburgh University Press, 1997.

Burrows, Edwin G., and Mike Wallace. *Gotham: A History of New York City to 1898.* New York: Oxford University Press, 1999.

Carpenter, George. *Calhoun is My Kingdom: The Sesquicentennial History of Calhoun County, Illinois.* Hardin: Calhoun Co. Historical Society, 2000.

Cobbett, William. *The Emigrant's Guide.* London: Published by author, 1829.

Davis, James E. *Frontier Illinois.* Bloomington, IN: Indiana University Press, 1998.

Erickson, Charlotte. *Invisible Immigrants: The Adaptation of English and Scottish Immigrants in 19th Century America.* Ithaca: Cornell University Press, 1972.

Foyster, Elizabeth and Christopher A. Whatley, eds. *A History of Everyday Life in Scotland, 1600 to 1800.* Edinburgh: Edinburgh University Press, 2011.

Greenberg, Amy S. *A Wicked War: Polk, Clay, Lincoln and the 1846 U.S. Invasion of Mexico.* New York: Vintage Books, 2012.

Langguth, A.J. *Driven West: Andrew Jackson and the Trail of Tears to the Civil War.* New York: Simon & Schuster, 2010.

Larkin, Jack. *The Reshaping of Everyday Life 1790-1840.* New York: Harper & Row, 1988.

Morris, Charles. *History of Pennsylvania.* Philadelphia: J.B. Lippincott & Company, 1913.

Niven, John. *John C. Calhoun and the Price of Union.* Baton Rouge: Louisiana State University Press, 1988.

Roberts, Alasdair. *America's First Great Depression: Economic Crisis and Political Disorder After the Panic of 1837.* Ithaca: Cornell University Press, 2012.

Rosenberg, Charles E. *The Cholera Years: The United States in 1832, 1849, and 1866.* Chicago: University of Chicago Press, 1987.

Shepard, Elihu H. *The Early History of St. Louis and Missouri.* St. Louis: Southwestern Book and Publishing Company, 1870.

Struever, Stuart, and Felicia Antonelli Holton. *Koster: Americans in Search of Their Prehistoric Past.* Long Grove, IL: Waveland Press, 1979.

Whyte, Donald. *Scottish Surnames.* Edinburgh: Birlinn Limited, 2000.

Wightman, Andy. *The Poor Had No Lawyers: Who Owns Scotland (And How They Got It).* Edinburgh: Birlinn Limited, 2013.

Acknowledgments

For as long as I can remember, Carroll Borrowman has worked diligently to track John's descendants in America. His enthusiasm for family history inspired this book.

Telling a story by connecting the dots relies on having enough dots to start with. Genealogical research from Stuart Borrowman, of Bathgate, Scotland, was the gateway to John's life in Dolphinton. Though I could find no connection between Stuart's line of Borrowmans and John's, this book would not be possible without him.

Michael Gallagher, at the Mitchell Library Archives in Glasgow, helped with access to material from the Mackenzie family archives regarding Dolphinton Estate. John Moore and Lorna Hyland, in the Archives of Merseyside Maritime Museum in Liverpool, fielded numerous questions about ships and sailing. The staff at Register House in Edinburgh dug out records of the Dolphinton Parish Kirk Session. Mike Fucella, Minister at Black Mount Parish Church, showed me an actual stool of repentance that was kept (though, thankfully, no longer used) at his home church in Biggar. Pamela and Andrew Taylor, owners of Meadowhead Farm, shared long ago construction drawings for Meadowhead and useful background about the sale of the Dolphinton Estate.

Barry Bonnett, with the Federal Bureau of Land Management, helped me understand how veterans of the War of 1812 claimed land within the Military Tract. Calhoun County records revealed many more dots. Rita Hagen, Anne Marie Johnson, and Rita Sievers of the Calhoun County Clerk's Office let me interrupt them time after time. Andy Borrowman drove me around northern Calhoun County and to the quarter section of land that John Borrowman owned. Andy sacrificed himself to a painful case of poison ivy as we searched for and found the cemetery where John is buried. Greg Miller was a ready source of perspective on farming in the early to mid-1800s.

After the dots were connected, Paul Menzel added life to the narrative with his ideas. David Dodd went above and beyond the call of duty as editor and in leading me by the hand through the publishing gauntlet. And finally, my wife, Martha, was a diligent researcher and reader whose notes in the margins of the manuscript always improved the story.

www.ingramcontent.com/pod-product-compliance
Lightning Source LLC
LaVergne TN
LVHW051704080426
835511LV00017B/2721